A Delicate And Precious Gift

A
DELICATE
And
PRECIOUS GIFT

One poet's view of the world

God has created a world filled with natural beauty and blessings. It is up to us to see this beauty and to thankfully recognize the blessings.

ROBERT LEE OBERST

XULON PRESS

Xulon Press
2301 Lucien Way #415
Maitland, FL 32751
407.339.4217
www.xulonpress.com

ISBN-13: 978-1-5456-6838-2

Dedication

I would like to dedicate this book to my mother, my wife Janet, and to God.

To my mother, my first teacher, who taught me to love God and His creation, and to love words and to love poetry.

Mom

Born on Mother's Day
I was a gift.
Your first child of five.
You gave us
So much for so long.
More than a life
Of love and faith
More than one song.
It's been thirty years now
Since you left us
For your heavenly reward.
Thanks Mom
For a life given
In service to the Lord.

To my wife, the love of my life, who has reflected God's love for me for over forty years in almost endless ways and who has made our family life a blessing filled reality.

Janet

I praise God:
For your many talents and skills
For your remarkable beauty and brains
For your willingness to serve others
For your humor and your wit
For your spiritual gifts and strengths
For your enduring love
For God, for me and for our family.
I pray for God to bless us
With many more days ahead together
And thank God for all the love we share
It is a little like a taste of heaven
And a breath of fresh air every day.

"To my God, the Creator of the universe, who came down from Heaven and sacrificed everything for me."

John 3:16

For God so loved the world that He gave His only begotten Son, that whoever believes in Him should not perish but have everlasting life.
New King James Version

Acknowledgements

S pecial thanks to my wife Janet, my sister Laurie Courage and my loving family for inspiring me to write my poems and helping me put this book together. I know that without Laurie's energy and expertise, this book would not have been possible.

Endorsements

I wish to thank Robert for his poetry submissions. His poems are easy to read and easy to follow the story. For someone like myself who never cared for poetry, his poems have helped me learn an appreciation for poetry.

I very much appreciate his sharing them with me; and I, in turn, publish them in our national monthly newsletter for our whole membership to enjoy. I always like being able to relate each of his poems to a season or an event.

–*Sheryl Bacon*,
Managing Editor, The Gardeners of America/Men's and Women's Garden Clubs of America

Robert Oberst's verse captures Syracuse in all of its seasonal disguises: biting winter, budding spring, languid summer, cool fall. Oberst's gentle observations of nature invite his readers to pause and appreciate the extraordinary, even spiritual beauty in our midst.

–*Marie Morelli*,
Newspaper Editor

It has been my pleasure over the years to publish Robert Oberst's poetry in the Adirondack Express. The poems are uplifting and thoughtful and sometimes provide a little chuckle. His words help one to focus on the things that are truly important like the feeling of fresh snow falling down, remembering the sacrifices of our vets and first responders, and the simple joys of spring.

Oberst's approach to the written word is thoughtful and welcome in this busy world.

–Lisa Monroe,
Editor, Adirondack Express

For decades, Bob Oberst has been a kind of spiritual witness to the quiet breathing, day to day life, of Syracuse- the city he loves with such devotion. This collection of his poetry, his gentle insights, offers testimony to the way he captures moments of quiet magnitude that become all too easy to miss.

–Sean Kirst,
Long Time Upstate Journalist and Storyteller

Table of Contents

Introduction

Webster's dictionary says a poem is a piece of writing (i.e. a composition) in verse...that is written in separate lines that often have repeated rhythm and sometimes rhyme. Thanks to my mother's love of reading and my college freshman English teacher Dr. Edward's focus on writing and poetry at New England College in New Hampshire I have spent many days enjoying reading and writing English.

Most of my writing has involved poems and letters to the editors that I have sent to a variety of publications covering a variety of subjects (from about 1970 to 2015). These publications included daily and weekly newspapers such as the City Eagle, Adirondack Express and the Empire State Farmer. I regularly wrote letters, poems and some columns for the Syracuse Herald Journal and the Syracuse Post Standard. For several years I wrote a paid column for a weekly local newspaper called the Solvay-Geddes Express. Occasionally I would contribute some of my photographs or post cards.to regional magazines or newspapers.

Some people who admire my poems asked me why I write poems and I tell them I write poems to capture some of the God-given beauty that is all around us and to recognize it with words or word pictures so others will also enjoy that beauty.

Fall

Time for a Change

Summer left town last night.
Without warning it took its hot misty
And sultry days and moved on.
The sun that came up this morning
In a bright blue sky
Had a fall chill about it
And the brisk wind said,
"It's time for a change".

Blue Sky

A postcard blue sky
Has kept my mind outside today.
Each yellow leaf that flipped and fell
In the warm fall breeze
Made me dream back
To all the autumns of my life
And I thanked God for today.

A Little More Time

A picture perfect deep blue sky
Filled the horizon today
Punctuated by a single puffy white cloud.
The crisp fall morning air
Gave way to a warm summer-like afternoon
As busy bees and flighty butterflies
Were given a little more time
To prepare for the winter days ahead.

Awesome Power

After a day of hard rain
That moved wet leaves on willing trees
To fall down and create a thick wet blanket
That covered everything on the ground,
There came a strong and cold north wind.
With this wind came swirling dark clouds
That moved multi-colored leaves
And all things not tied down from here to there.
This whistling wind pushed and pulled.
It rolled and slid objects and people.
It pelted and pushed rain drops, snowflakes and hail.
It animated large puffy clouds and small stringy clouds.
It whipped flags and wires.
It bent over young trees and twisted their branches.
It created drifts of leaves
From places where they were piled up
To places where they will soon drift.
This mighty wind was just another reminder
Of the awesome power and majesty of God, our Creator
And also, a reminder of the very changeable days
In the season to come.

Along for The Ride

Today,
While others went
About their business,
I, not knowing any better,
Spent a minute looking up
Through brightly colored leaves
At a flock of geese
As they honked their way
Across my few feet of sky.
So slowly did they fly,
My neck stiffened
As I watched small groups
Of three or four birds
Move from place to place
In their changing V-formation.
On days like this
I wish that I could
Go along just for a ride.

Beauty All Around

Ever watch a leaf float by
Your window on a windy day?
See how lightly it does fly
Like time it quickly drifts away.
See the trees move to and fro
Hoping their treasure won't let go?
Hear that wild wind sound
As red leaves blow round and round?
Look at the clouds as they go by
In the deep blue sea, we call the sky.
If you see beauty all around
Then you know why leaves abound.

Crisp Fall Air

Crisp fall air
Stirs inside of me
Memories of falling leaves
And stormy lakes,
Of apple-filled trees
And geese passing south,
Of fluffy white clouds
Against a deep blue sky,
Of plump pumpkins
And curious chipmunks
Of fresh-squeezed cider
And many-colored hills,
And of God,
Who made them all.

Chill

A winter-like chill arrived last night
With a brisk wind for a friend.
I didn't mind those mild fall days
That never seemed to end.
But chilled I'll be for a few "short" months
When that friend of spring, the warm sun
will return again.

Tonight

Rain in a torrent, pouring
Splashing, dripping, crashing
Outpouring in darkness
Alive and different,
Yet rhythmically silent.
Leaves reluctant to go–
Falling, blowing,
Shining in the street light glow
Dying quietly together.
Ground swelling with fluidity
And strange blanketed beauty
Drowning in abundance…
Night all encompassing
But soon to come
The white in the night.

Frosty Curtain

Today
As the sun moved across a deep blue afternoon sky
It warmed the crisp fall air.
Bright red and yellow leaves that covered so many
Neighborhood trees fell in the gentle autumn breeze.
Some fall-blooming flowers still looked especially vigorous
With last week's rain and this week's cool air.
Yet there is a different kind of beauty to come
When a hard frost will coat every flower and green plant
And like the final curtain of a long running popular play
A frosty curtain of white will descend on this year's
Long running growing season's finale.
What a blessing!

Fall Afternoon

I see so much beauty all around
On a warm early fall afternoon
With a hazy green hill looking down on me
And rows of brown and green corn just
Standing there moving with the breeze.

The crickets are so loud they almost block
Out the sounds of cows making merry
Or the sound of a farmer's tractor working fields.
The warm sun on my face is perfectly balanced
With a touch of cool fall air at my back.

My old Model "A" Ford bounces and sways
Along empty country roads that seem to have been made for it
And I see God in every tree, hear Him in every sound,
Feel Him in every breeze.

© Robert Oberst

Especially Thankful

Why Thanksgiving?
Why do Americans
Celebrate this day?
It's their history.
A history of
Struggles and survival
Of physical and spiritual battles
Against elements and enemies.
A history of faith, hope,
Sacrifice and thanksgiving.
To whom
Are Americans thankful?
Some are not thankful to anyone.
But people of faith
Thank their Creator, God,
Not just for earth, moon and sky
But for each other
And for the cornucopia
Of spiritual gifts
And blessings that make us
Who we are.
This thankfulness
Is not limited to one day.
It carries believers
Past good days and bad
And past days of plenty or want
To rejoice and be glad
And to be especially thankful.

Soon

The wind is blowing strong tonight
Brittle trees bend and twist.
Melting snow drips down every roof
Yet the air seems uncommonly cold.
A dog howls not far away
And winter is soon here.

Last Flower

Last night
A hard frost coated each plant
And blade of grass.
Bright yellow petals
And still green leaves
Slept with an icy blanket
And in the morning sun
They glistened and sparkled
One last time before
They were gone.

Our Friendly Garden

The soft warm sound of music
Fills our home today
As the look of a bright sun-filled fall afternoon
fills our backyard picture window.
Orange and red maple leaves mixed
with yesterday's green ones
hang on willowy branches.

Dark green grass is covered
With "orange freckles"
And bright yellow marigolds
Still stand tall along the border
Of our friendly garden.

One Last Time

This morning a brilliant sun
Came up in a cold blue sky.
The farmer's market was
Full of so many good things
But the cold wind
Made us move quickly
With our apples, cider and fresh pie.
Blowing leaves of many colors
Still moved in every direction
As I mowed the lawn
One last time.
We started up the old Ford Model "A"
And took it for a neighborhood spin.
Gradually the blue sky
Filled with dark clouds
And turned to gray
Then a strong wind
Filled the air with snow.
By evening the snow was everywhere
And the snow-covered car looked like
Some old post card view
As we pulled into the garage
On this, the last real day of fall.

Winter

Alone

The hours passed
On a seeming endless country road
And it made me very tired.
Although I was alone
Many thoughts filled my mind.
The snow-covered mountain road
Blended with the rain and fog covered air.
I wondered where I was
Or how long it would take me to get where I was going
Or even if I should have stayed where I was yesterday.
Then through the fog, close by the side of the road
A doe stood and looked at me.
Her head followed me as I passed
And she looked as much lost in the fog as I was
But her face seemed friendly.
It was a that moment that I was reminded
That with God I'm never really alone.

Days to Come

This morning a wet snow washed down
From a cold rain laden sky.
Some flakes stuck to some red leaves
And spent flowers,
While others for a short time,
Covered the dark green grass
With a wet white blanket
Giving us a small taste
Of the days to come.

Lost in The White

White in the night
Wind in the air
Snow all around
Dark everywhere.
Crackling fire
Keeps us warm
But outside
Black trees
Are lost in the white.

Snow Moon

This afternoon a full moon
Hung in the clear blue sky,
As a wave of cotton-like clouds
Passed over it.
This face of gray was surrounded
With a crystal light halo
Like a beautiful seashell
Washed over by a salty flood.
Then the snow moon was gone.

Snow

Snow, unsure of itself,
Fell tonight on the pale white street
With the dripping sound of rain.
Coarse and granular beads
Bouncing like marbles
More like rain than snow
In the bitter cold
Gave my hand a bite.
And I thanked God
For the warm place we call home.

Little Sign

Fluffy white flakes of silent sounding snow
Are falling on the street outside my window.
They blanket every branch of every tree,
Clothe every dark thing in white
And make it hard to see.

Like little cotton drops
The snow slips
Through branches and telephone lines
Past rows of roof tops and isles of icicles
Down, down and around.

The shoveled path I made a while ago
Has filled with new white fallen snow
But I didn't mind this fluff from above
For each day it falls it makes
The ground seem new
And shows me a little sign of God's love.

Thaw

A December thaw
Caught us by surprise
With a rush of mild air,
Some shower filled days
And even a bit of bright sun.
After so many weekends
Of cold air and all kinds of snow
As well as ice coated spots
And even a white out or two,
We know that spring is months away
But we thank God
Even for one mild spring-like day
At the start of winter.

Endure

Blue sky and sunshine
Were everywhere today
As yesterday's endless snow flurries
Took a break
And puffs of white smoke
Drifted up from many smoke stacks
Across the horizon.
The sun-dried highway
Turned a salty white
As so many cars and busses
Transported their owners
To work, to school and other places.
And the American flag on top
Of our town's tallest building
Waved in a stiff north breeze.
Some of us are willing to endure
A below zero day or two
In exchange for a chance to see
And appreciate a sunny day
In the middle of January
Even as we dream
Of spring days ahead.

Wild Ride

This winter has been a long and wild
Roller coaster ride in Central New York.
From early and heavy snows
To days of fast thaws,
From bitter cold winds
To mild rain-filled afternoons,
From almost instant melt downs and flooding
To "wind burst" storms that leveled many trees.
We can be thankful
That memories of this winter
Will soon melt away into spring
And the wild ride will be
Over for another year.

It's Cold

Cold hands and feet
Cold face and ears
Cold homes and cars
Cold eyes and tears.
Frozen cars that don't start.
Frozen pipes that burst
When they freeze.
Salt that turns snow to grease
Especially at zero degrees.
Schools that are closed
With kids at home
But it's so cold
They do not roam.
Wind-chill is low
But snow piles high.
How cold can it be
And still have folks get by?
Cold wind
Cold air
Cold breath
Out there.
Can't wait
For the day
Several months away
When we all can rejoice
With a warm and loud voice
That spring is really here!

Winter Cheer

Why shovel that snow?
Eventually it will melt you know!
Why push, scrape and lift
Just to move that drift?
Why clear that way
When you could wait another day?
Who cares if the mail can't get through?
Or if the newspaper gets lost too?
Who cares if the car gets stuck
And has to be pulled out by a AAA truck?
Who cares if people have to walk in the street
Because your sidewalk is far from neat?
Why not care for walking folks, my friend
And shovel your driveway and sidewalk to the end?
Or you could pay a youngster to do a job or two?
It will make your street better all winter through.
And if you had some energy to spare
Why not shovel a neighbor's walk here and there?
So when the snow is gone for another year
You will know that you did your best
To bring your neighbors some real winter cheer!

Winter Air

Cold winter air
Stirs inside of me
Memories of clear blue skies
And hills blanketed in white;
Of soft fluffy snow flakes
And evergreen branches bent low;
Of cheerful Chickadees
Who take seeds from my hand;
Of frozen waterfalls
And ice-covered lakes;
Of hungry squirrels
Who dig everywhere;
And of God
Who made them all.

© Robert Oberst

My Winter Garden

Just before the first frost comes to visit our yard,
It's time to move my two small lemon trees inside
To my winter garden where they share a spot along
A large south-facing window with a potpourri of plants:
Ivy Geranium, Norfolk Island pine tree, crown of thorns,
English ivy, asparagus fern, Amaryllis bulb, jade plant,
Swedish ivy, philodendron, spider plant,
Moses-in-the-bulrushes, African violet, crown of thorns'
Strawberry begonias and even some basil.
Our cat hardly has room to squeeze into her sun-warmed
Window sill spot next to the plant stand with so many plants.
As she brushes past the crown of thorns it brushes her hair,
And she runs when I water the plants too much
Or spray a fine warm mist over so many green leaves.
In fall most of my indoor garden rests,
In late winter it starts to grow again,
And by early spring it explodes with new growth,
Thanks to a little fertilizer and lots of sun.
My winter garden doesn't take a lot of room
But it stays green even as the piles of snow
And so many rude icicles grow and grow.
It's nice to have a winter garden
But it is a real blessing to rejoice on the day
When my lemon trees can once again return
To their summer home in a warm spot
Outside in my summer garden.

Night Garden in Winter

Our Douglas Fir branches are bent really low
Pointed toward the ground because of the snow.
The garden is covered with a blanket of white
And not even the neighbor's cat cuts through our yard tonight.
October's pumpkins still sit out in the cold
But with each thaw their faces grow less bold.
The old water pump stands proud and tall
But its brown wooden bucket is full of ice, that's all.
A cold full moon lights up the land
And some tree shadows look like a mighty big hand.
The kale in the garden still looks green
But because it's frozen it still makes a good scene.
Our carrots are buried under the frost
Perhaps they'll still be good in spring and won't be lost.
Our night garden in winter is a beautiful thing
But I'm already counting the days until spring.

Something Special

There is something very special about
How even the most modest residential street
Is almost transformed back in time by a heavy snowfall
Into an old-fashioned post card winter scene.
The snow covers majestic area trees
As well as little neighborhood imperfections
In a blanket of white
And the sounds of human activity are centered indoors.
As the cold settles in
There is a winter silence that fills the air
Only broken by the muffled noise of a passing car
Or the crunchy sound of people walking by in the snow.
You can almost imagine a horse drawn sleigh
Going by on a dark night.
Yards are separated by growing piles of white
Even as neighbors get reacquainted when they
Shovel side by side or shovel a neighbor's yard.
The pace of life slows down a bit as people
Spend more time closer to home with their families.
It is so important to appreciate the many
God given blessings all around us
Even in the middle of a very snowy winter.

Reason

The reason for the season
Is not the thousands of lights
Not the endless decorated green trees.
It is not the countless sales or parties
Nor the frantic pace
Of Christmas shopping and doing.
For Christians it is:
The child born as a gift
From our loving Creator God
To all who accept His love.

Splendid Isolation

Splendid isolation
With no one near
Out in the country
With only God to hear
My humble prayer of thanks.
Snow coming down
Wind blowing 'round
Fire burning low
Winter won't let go.
But in a while His spring
(Such a pretty thing)
Will be here
And splendid isolation
Will melt away
For another year.

No Longer Free

Tonight, stars abound and the moon fills the horizon
With light but the sky is not clear.
Gray soot rises from area smoke stacks
And is carried to neighboring homes
For people to breathe.
No one is untouched.
The dust finds its way into each house.
The snow turns dirty gray.
Windows are bathed in grime.
Auto and truck exhaust add their share
To an evening of acid fog.
When will we realize that the air
We breathe is no longer free?

Winter Is Just Teasing Us

Sweet smell of thaw with swishy pools
And endless street rivers
Is everywhere today.
Not waiting for its January time this year.
The thaw has come and gone many times.
It teases us to think spring is near
With mild air and bright sun filled blue sky
When we know winter is just
Hiding out behind the barn.

First Hint

Each tree is dressed in winter wear:
A mantle of soft white
As a gusty wind
Shakes the dust of snow
From willing branches.
Crows cry out in a dense pine woods
And in the distance
The sound of wind
Whistling through bare branches
Grows loud.
A cold sun shines through trees
And reflects off the frozen lake
That waits for more winter,
But even as we look
For the first hint of spring
The days grow longer.

This Year

From November to April
Snowflakes filled the air this year.
Though lately orange was our
Color not white.
Winter storms were not limited to snow.
We had our share of rain and ice,
Thaws and freezes.
Once we even had a "wind burst"
That took many of our best evergreen trees.
Perhaps this is the year for us
To be extra thankful for even a single
Sun-filled spring afternoon
Or for a week of blooming spring flowers
Especially in this place called Syracuse.

Spring

Even One

This afternoon two seasons clashed
When April gave up a day to March.
Snow drops fell down and daffodils were shocked
By the sudden surprise attack.
All at once rows of green flower stems
Stood soldier neat surrounded and
In sharp contrast to a new blanket of white.
Song birds spoiled by several mild days and spring rains
Searched harder for something to eat.
We are sent days like today by God to help us
Appreciate the varied beauty of spring in Central New York
Especially when even one
Warm sunny day appears.

Hope!

The sun says "It's spring".
Such a warm thing
As birds sing an April song.
The cold March wind still blows
But each tree knows
It's time to start
To point its branches
Toward the sun.
A fly buzzed by me just now
And, you know, I was happy to see it
Though by August
I will want to see it gone.
Such blue-sky days like today
Were made by God
To show us how eternal hope is.

Waterfall

This morning a great waterfall
Washed down from a gray sky.
It woke me with a gentle hand
And then lulled me back to sleep
With its constant rhythm.
The splashy echo of water on stone walks
Mixed with dull sounds of rain on trees
Seemed to deaden all other sounds.
Although my garden was ever so saturated
I still thank God for the rain.

This Place

Brown grass
And sunbaked soil turned to dust
Marked the first day of spring this year.
No heavy spring rains washed away winter's salt
And roadside soil is still edged in white.
Garden plants and even trees not watered
Have wilted after so many long hot days
And squirrels are working overtime
Looking for vegetation that has moisture in it.
Even hardy weeds that only need a sprinkle are dormant.
Perhaps this is the year
For us to learn to be thankful
For even a single passing shower
Especially in this place called Syracuse.

Spring Air

Brisk spring air
Stirs inside of me
Memories of snow drops and crocuses
Pushing up through crusty snow,
Of swelling lilac buds
And returning robins
Of hard rains
That wash away winter grime,
Of hyperactive squirrels
Who dig in every corner of our yard,
Of the fertile soil in the garden
Ready for another growing season,
And of God
Who made them all.

Relentless Rain

Wet, misty, relentless, spotty,
Clammy, drippy, raw, cold,
Steamy or mushy,
Yet it fills endless life-giving
Pools, rivers and streams.
It comes quietly without warning
In a mist or downpour.
It comes with wind,
Lightning and thunder.
It washes away yesterday
And gives moisture for tomorrow.
Most of all, as people out west
Often pray for rain
It makes many people in Central New York
Grateful not only for water
But especially thankful
For every sun-filled day we have.
What a blessing.

Wet and Green

Wet and green
This spring time scene
With streets so clean
And birds serene.
Flowers there
Don't seem to care
If sun won't dare
Come out a hair.
Bustling buds
And wiggling worms
Make known a day in spring.

Sweet Spring Rain

Sweet spring rain falls
Outside my window.
It splashes and drips
As it covers the ground
With pools of clear water.
The air is warm and moist
And I would have thought
It to be summer
If I didn't see only new green leaves
On just a few trees.
How beautiful for God to renew
So many things in spring.

LEWIS PARK

CITY OF SYRACUSE

DEPARTMENT OF
PARKS & RECREATION

Spring in Our Neighborhood

It's baseball time in Lewis Park.
Nick's ice cream store is open on Avery Ave.
And tree buds are swelling at Pass' field.
Young people are playing golf again at Burnet Park
And zoo sounds of birds and beasts
Can be heard for blocks.
The green light is still on top at Tompkins Street
And flags still wave at Tipp Hill Park.
Coleman's Restaurant still has great corned beef
And the train from Carousel Station
Is back on track to downtown.
Daffodils are everywhere
As spring rains pass
And neighbors say, "We are ready".

Bloom Fest

Unlike last spring
With its late cold frosty days
This year has been
A festival of blossoms
With not just snowdrops
And crocus plants,
Pansies, irises, daffodils and tulips
But also, yards full of forsythia,
Rhododendron, spirea and lilac flowers
As well as streets lined with bloom-filled redbud,
Dogwood, crabapple, cherry and pear trees.
Praise God, especially for
The festival of flowers this spring!

Spring in Central NY

White, cold and windy
Then white, wet and bright
Then white, bright and muddy
Then wet, brown and waterlogged
Then wet, green and…even sunny!

In Loving Memory

h

sh

re.

y
ne
ain
will live on.
ill complain
s and roads
nd yards
But this is the time to rake up the loads
Before green grass starts to grow
And has to be mowed.

So, let's not wait
For just one special day
To bag up winter's waste
And have it taken away
With real and timely haste.
Let's give real meaning
To the beautiful results
Of a good neighborhood
Spring-cleaning.

This May

This year May borrowed many days from June.
Flowers that bloomed weeks early
Lasted for more than their usual time,
But as the days of warm sun continued
The grass that some folks cut too short
Turned brown and newly planted flower beds went dry.
Yet while some people couldn't get enough sun-filled days
Many farmers and gardeners prayed for some rain
And by the last day of May
Rain finally came with wind and storms.

Superbells

One day last spring
Our neighbors gave our family a hanging basket
Of "Superbells" (Hybrid Calibrachoa)
To hang by our front door.
While some of these petunia-like miniatures
Lost some luster over time
New flower buds took their place.
They tolerated hot sun, strong winds, hard rain
And even a squirrel attack.
Every day we enjoyed each flower's beauty.
Then late one special sun-filled afternoon
Our family was blessed by a chance
To enjoy viewing a rare sight in our city garden:
A humming bird lingering for a visit
To flower after flower in our basket.
Then in an instant the bird was gone.
Later I made a special note
To look for more "Superbells"
For our yard next spring
And to even give some to a neighbor.

Rebirth

Rain in a shower
Drips and splashes away
All of yesterday's snow.
It taps on my window
Every now and then
To tell me spring is in the air.
The quiet white evenings of winter
Have been replaced by
The dark splashy flood of spring.
It seems that this is the moment
All God's creatures
Are awaiting a new rebirth.

Peepers

To sing in spring
Is my favorite thing
When skies sparkle
And leaves rustle
When sunshine glistens
And people listen
To birds and peepers and things
When two people walk together
Hand in hand as one.

Forty Days

Forty Days
To sing the praise
Of One who died
And then did rise
Up from the dead
To save us from ourselves.

Forty days
This season of Lent
To stop our world
And really repent
Of sinful ways.

Forty days
To come to the place
Where sorrow is gone
And we can rejoice
To live with our
Mighty risen Lord.

Easter

Easter.
For Christians
What does it mean?
Spring?
Jelly beans?
Chocolate bunnies?
Why not a rebirth of hope?
A new beginning?

A remembrance of one death
Over 2000 years ago

That ended with a resurrection
And that can lead all who believe
To eternal life.
Rejoice and be glad!

Elation at Creation

Each day
The light stays a little longer
And the sun is a little stronger.
The snow piles retreat
And it is really neat
To watch the little signs
Of change if we open our minds
With eyes that see
And focus, or sadly be
Overwhelmed by past memories
Of cold nights but look ahead
To bursting buds and song birds in flight.
Even on very cold sun-filled days
It is amazing to see all the ways
That the little signs of spring
Eventually are transformed
Into a cornucopia of growing things
And also grow into a feeling of elation
At the great beauty of all God's creation.

This Place Called Country

The Moonlight
Was like a street light,
Shining without stars
In the foggy night.
The blanket-like mist
Kissed A farmer's field
As I passed through patches
On a rural mountain road
In this place called country

Summer

© Robert Oberst

Single Day

Without warning summer-like air
Invaded our yard this week.
Chilly nights and cool gray afternoons
Gave way to days of brilliant sunshine,
Blue sky and warm moist air.
Even the cold water in our newly filled kiddie pool
Quickly turned warm with the noon sun.
Our tomato and pepper plants seem to explode with growth
Out of the ground with the rush of warm air.
And dozens of daylilies seemed almost ready
For their one day of glory.
The new rye grass I planted over those bare lawn spots
Has become lush and green now and impatiens
Now paint the yard with many colors.
It is a very special God given gift
To experience and appreciate the beauty
Of even a single day in early summer.

Summer Rain

The first summer rain fell tonight
Just as the light of day
Was drifting away.
Trees with newly grown leaves
Seemed to reach out and touch the dark sky
As water rushed over pointed roofs
And poured down countless mini water falls
To grass and streets below.
The lawn soaked up this damp deluge
And waited for more
And I thanked God for the rain.

Safe Harbor

(At the Harbor Brook Retention Basin)

On a recent sun-filled
Sunday afternoon
My family and I
Found a large green area
In which to have a picnic.
It was not far from our city home
And it had a clear stream
That ran past the spot.
After we ate our lunch
We walked along the brook.
As we walked, we saw
Several Mallard ducks as they
Moved along the stream banks
In search of a meal.
We also watched schools of minnows
Swim among the shore plants.
Later, I discovered deer tracks
In the shore mud

That marked a deer crossing.
There were grassy areas
And marsh grass with willow and other trees.
Across a heavily traveled road
We walked to a large wetland
Full of plants and birds.
One of our children saw a hawk
On the ground eating a garden snake
And there were many signs of woodchuck
Activity in many spots.
It was a real pleasure for our family to visit
And enjoy this natural green and wildlife filled area
Even on the edge of a place called Syracuse.

Complain About the Rain

Wind and rain
Wind and rain
After such a hot dry summer
How can we complain?
Wet grass and leaves
Wet grass and leaves
After so many dry leaves and plants
How can we grieve?
Puddles and streams
Puddles and streams
As they steadily fill up
It's a good time to dream.
As a new sunny morning comes again
We rejoice for sure
And still thank God for the rain.

© Robert Oberst

Sunset Fire Light

The evening sky is on fire
As a brilliant sun
Pushes its rays
Through blanket-like clouds.
Bits of fire light
Burn the underside of blue-black clouds
And in gold leaf outline others.
Gold turns pink
And then the sun is gone.

But We Are Thankful

A crisp blue sky
Outlined by a few puffy white clouds
Filled the moist air this morning.
Neighborhood birds were especially loud
As robins sought out their breakfast
On the wet grass.
Yesterday's rain showers
That passed through our area
Washed away summer dust
And watered many plants
In our already dry summer garden.
Yet it was hard to tell
Which plants had grown the most
In just that single day.
It was an unexpected God given blessing
To have warm July borrow
A cool day from September
But we are thankful.

Fireflies and Rain

After a soaking summer thunder shower
 Washed over a parched land,
As well as so many thirsty plants
And interrupted our family picnic,
We were greatly impressed
With the sight of a field of tall grass
. Filled with hundreds of moving fireflies
Like a natural fireworks display
Next to a lake, explorers called Champlain.
These lightening bugs seemed to celebrate
The return of moisture to the land
(Even as far off lightning flashes still lit up the sky)
And we thanked God for the beauty
Of His creation especially for fireflies and rain.

Natural Feeder

The tall man-sized sunflower plant
Just outside our kitchen window
Is blooming now.

Not content to have just one blossom,
Our plant will have many soon.
But for now, the one bright flower
Points our way.

When the flower fades,
We will let the plant stand
And then bow its head.
And if the squirrels don't get it first
A couple of nearby Cardinals
Will get their breakfast
Outside our window
For at least a week or so,
And we won't mind at all.

Summer Shower

Caught up in a summer shower
Watching branches twist and turn
Watching temporary rivers surge
Watching lightening flash across the sky
And feeling the sound of thunder
Against our window pane
Then listening to the crackle-filled air
So close you can almost taste the current.
Seeing new streams and new ponds of clear water
Alive with so many drops and bubbles
As green plants drink their fill.
It is a privilege to witness even this part
Of God's mystifying creation.

Warm Summer Air

Warm summer air
Stirs inside of me
Memories of dark woods
And quiet lakes,
Of tall trees
And singing birds,
Of fluffy clouds
And green mountains,
Of crashing waterfalls
And curious chipmunks,
Of smelly skunks
And exploring raccoons,
Of hungry young rabbits,
And air-born wild turkeys,
And of God
Who made them all.

Search the Waters

After a morning filled with brilliant warm sun
Butterflies and bees, flowers and singing.
A cold, gusty wind moved calm
Lake waters to grow restless.
Trees, still warm from the morning sun,
Were shook until they gave up
Their acorns and yellow leaves.
Blue sky clinging to a golden sun
Was covered with a cotton-lined
Blanket of clouds as distant hills grew
Misty and then were gone.
White caps covered a gray sea
And sea gulls searched for food.
On days like today, God,
The Creator, changes
Sleepy lakes into restless seas
To remind us who is the author of all life.

Our Old Maple Tree

For a hundred years
You stood between our little house and the street
You grew and grew until you were taller than our home.
In summer you gave us cool shade.
In fall your red and yellow leaves filled the air.
In winter you kept the snow plow off our porch.
In spring the birds filled your tall branches.
From time to time some branches died
But I fed you in spring
And planted daylilies at your feet.
I even put burlap along the street
To keep the road, salt off your sugar maple roots.
The Labor Day storm took you down
And you landed on our roof.

I knew it was your time
But I will really miss you
Especially when spring comes again.
So I'll plant another tree in your place
But it won't be the same.

Why Garden?

Whether you only have a little time
Or many free hours;
Whether you only have a single clay pot
Or an acre of land;
Whether your yard has only
Part shade for a few hours
Or many hours of full sun;
Whether it rains for 100 days
A year where you call home
Or you live in a desert;
You can still have a garden.
Whether you have an inside
Or an outside place to grow plants
You can have a real chance to see
A variety of plants grow and even bloom.
Although almost any place can be your garden
From a small plot, an old oak bucket
Or even a Styrofoam cup
Some of your attempts to grow plants will fail.
But with some persistence and
A willingness to learn and work
As well as some help
 From the original Master Gardener
Your garden will grow and even thrive.
Keep planting!

Questions

What is it that draws people to a lake shore?
Or to places where land meets water?
What makes us want to hear and enjoy the
Sounds of waves washing over rocks
Or the sound of offshore wind whistling past trees?
Why do we enjoy the songs of shore birds
And gull cries intermingling at first light?

Is it the sight of water in an ever-changing state?
One day like glistening glass, the next day like a raging sea?
Is it the fresh fragrant air and the varied wildlife
And greenery that are so abundant?

Could it be that at this place we are reminded how special yet
Fragile all life is, and how we are part of God's won-
der-filled creation?

© Robert Oberst

Glenwood

Last Sunday morning
As we drove along a road called Glenwood
And passed a sign that said," Wildlife Safety Zone"
A young doe looked up from her morning meal.

She knew we meant no harm
So, she continued to eat along the side of the road.
We were reminded of God's creation
Even in this place called Syracuse.

© Robert Oberst

Fourth of July

Fourth of July
What does it mean?
Celebration?
Next vacation?
Contemplation
Of why we as a country exist?
What did it cost for our freedom?
It wasn't free.
There was a price to pay
In lives, wealth and power.
We fought and died.
We built and defended.
We hammered out laws.
We made mistakes and corrected them.

Our motto was E Pluribus Unum-
Out of many one.
We believed in rights that were
Endowed by our Creator
So we wrote on our currency,
"In God We Trust"
And we said on our pledge,
"Under God".
But if we still believe in America
And we want this country
To continue as a free land
We must still work hard together
To preserve, protect and defend
The beliefs that built this country
Even as we sing and say again the
the words of God Bless America.

Sky Bright (summer 1967)

The Newark sky is bright with fire,
People running, cars burning
Windows broken, sides taken.
A fire engine stops to fight a fire
But troopers with weapons pointed skyward
Carefully check rooftops first for snipers
And after a time, firemen begin their work…
Buildings and cars burn on.

Garden Power

This summer with its lack of rain
And numbing days of 90 degrees
Has been a real test for avid gardeners.
Even late into spring
Frosty nights kept gardeners
From planting those tender annuals.
Hardy bulbs and perennials did fine
As cool nights made their flowers
Last and last, yet some did suffer
A bit from the cold.
When summer really arrived
The June heat cooked some
Young plants right where they were
Planted long before they could grow.
But there were summer plants
That thrived and bloomed.
These were potted plants
That were watered and fed
Very regularly.

Gardens too that were fed
And regularly watered really thrived.
What a real blessing to go a few steps
From your backyard door
And pick fresh peas, spinach, corn or tomatoes
As you sit down to some of your own home-grown food
And even set your table with flowers from your own garden.

© Robert Oberst

Warm

A warm summer breeze
Drifts through green trees
As the bright sun
Sends folks out for fun
And robins hunt for a meal with class
On a light green blanket of just cut grass.
A blue jay calls through so many places
Then flies past numerous hidden spaces.
A chipmunk scampers along its way
On this special day.

Forever Changed: Labor Day
Storm 9/7/98

We missed it…
After seven days of no cold
To keep food fresh
Of no heat to cook inside
Of no fans to cool our home
Of no more clean clothes.
We miss them.
Oh, it was nice to eat by oil lamp light
And spend family time looking out at the stars.
Walks in the neighborhood were a real challenge
With all the wires down or broken.
It was nice to listen to the crickets
Until all the area generators started up.
We hope that neighbors helping neighbors will continue
Now that the lights are on again
And we have the power back
But our neighborhood is forever changed
As we already miss so many tall trees
Yet, we will plant more for the generation to come.

Little Signs

The dogwood trees in our yard have already set their
Buds for next spring's blossoms,
While a red tint has appeared on the
Leaves of our neighbor's burning bushes.
We freed our last monarch butterfly
Just as we ran out of milkweed plants
To feed any more caterpillars.
Our last sunflower has bloomed and
All the cherry tomatoes in the garden
Have been picked and eaten.

Many leaves are already falling
Off our cherry tree but our rose of Sharon bushes
Still have a few blooms on them.
Many daylily leaves, after turning brown in summer,
Have been replaced by new green ones
Even as mums are just starting to show their best colors.
The tall yellow Jerusalem Artichokes are in full bloom.
It is a God given blessing to see and appreciate
The little signs that point the way
To the beauty of the fall season ahead.

Earlier Then You Expect

It seems that some signs of fall
Come earlier then you expect:
One summer day the corn is growing tall
And tomatoes are mostly still green.
The sunflower plant heads are still
Following the sun across the sky.
The grass has stopped growing
And turned light brown.

Then it happens:
A heavy late summer rain washes over the land
And overnight it awakens or transforms
So many green plants into a new season.
The corn is ready to harvest.
Tomatoes are ready to pick.
Sunflowers fix their gaze on one spot
And then bend their heads down.
The grass turns quickly green and starts to grow again.
Mums have started to bloom and the kale is beginning to change color.
Tall artichoke plants are starting to show their "wild sunflowers".
And the beauty of God's creation is still evident
At the very end of summer and the beginning of fall.

Garden Visitor

Some zinnias I bought
At the farmer's market in late spring
Grew unusually tall in my raised bed
City garden this year.
In a summer filled with warmth and sun
And even some rain
They grew and grew as if to compete
With my giant sunflowers
To over a foot tall.
Butterflies visited them
Often on sunny days
Yet on one extra special afternoon
I watched as a lone hummingbird
Visited the very tallest zinnia flower
And just then I made a mental note
To save some space in my garden
For some zinnias again next year.

Sweet Regret

When the gentle breeze of fall stirs fields of dry corn
And the air trades the hot dry afternoons of summer
For the cool moist evenings of autumn
There is a feeling of loss.
Many leaves that were once deep green
Have turned yellow or brown
And now they are punctured with insect holes.
Numerous lawns have dried up and
Turned into brown hay fields
Yet the air is filled with change.
Lazy summer afternoons,
When time seems to stand still,
Will soon be replaced with busy fall days
When there will be little time to stop the clock.
But hope springs eternal
And autumn colors are yet to come.
It is with sweet regret we will, in a while,
Say goodbye to summer.

Faith

© Robert Oberst

A Delicate and Precious Gift

A flower is a poem
With the words
Written on the petals
And the rhyme in the fragrance.
It is a delicate and precious
Gift from God.

I Am

I am the sky.
I am the snow.
I am the wind,
And the rain you know.
I fly with the birds
And run with the deer.
I walk with people everywhere.
I offer the gift of faith
To believe and follow me.
For I am God the Almighty.

Lord

Lord,
Teach us to write with your hands
To see with your eyes;
To speak with your voice;
To love with your heart;
Teach us to be as your servants.

Benediction

May the peace of Jesus Christ
Go with you every day.
May His word walk by your side
And may His Spirit with you pray.
May His love surround you.
May His will be done.
May his grace astound you
As we all become as one.

His Way

He has a way of telling you which way is up.
Day by day you feel His presence.
When you do as He commands
He lets you know that He is pleased.
He makes you realize the beauty of every day
And not just the sun-filled ones.
He gives you greater insight into
His word as you read
And even with the depth of complexity
Understanding increases.

Listening

Walking I realized how far I had to go.
Talking I saw how little I know.
Writing I knew how limited my gift.
Listening I see the way to lift…
God's will above my own!

Precious Day

Each second passes
And with it goes
One beam of natural light.
Slowly at first
But then, as if from behind
Your back, darkness leaps out
And then before you know it
The night envelops you
And you have lost another precious day.
We need to greatly appreciate
This special gift from God.

Majesty

Threatening billows of ominous clouds
Fill this part of sky
As clouds of dust sweep along the ground
And warm air rushes by my window.
Light flashes toward the heated ground
And countless drops of water fall from the sky.
The majesty and power of God is everywhere-
Evident, especially on days like today.

Gratitude

We are thankful for:
Life, love and family
For home, friends and neighbors
For our work, our home
And for bad as well as good days
For sun, rain and even snow
And for green gardens
For rolling hills
Productive farms
And restless lakes
For wildlife, plants
And trees
But most of all
For God, our loving Creator
And for all His creation.

A Special God Given Blessing

Ever so quietly,
The growing season left us.
While we were asleep,
The crickets stopped their song and
When the sun came up,
A frosty white blanket
Covered the flowers out back
With an icy glaze.
Heavy, cold air moved
Red and yellow leaves
Past our window.
A clear blue sky
Seasoned with a few puffy clouds
Brought back memories
Of many autumn days.
The smell of cold apples
On the front porch
And the taste of apple-cinnamon pancakes
With maple syrup from the kitchen
Mixed with the familiar feel of an old flannel shirt
I wore as I walked out
To check the garden.
It is a God given blessing
To be alive
On days like today.

Lord and Father

It is so easy to be thankful for your many gifts,
When I lay looking at a cotton white sky
Filled with patches of blue;
When I roll in a blanket of crispy
Crunchy brown leaves;
When I notice a bee looking for
A late summer blossom;
When I hear thousands of rustling
Weather-beaten leaves
Move with the wind.
It seems that I could sleep a hundred days
On afternoons like this.
Thank you, Lord,
For all your countless blessings!

More Questions

Have you heard that, "Jesus loves you!"?
Have you listened to His call?
Have you felt His healing power
And believed it all?
Did you know that He gave
His body and blood
To set all men free
And that He will come again
For all the world to see?

God's Love

Washing over me
Like a flood of rain drops
That come in a downpour -
God's love
Covers me with a feeling of wellbeing.
His Spirit fills my soul with grace
Washing away my sins and shortcomings.
He forgives me and renews my heart
And gives me energy and hope for tomorrow.
Thank You Lord!

His Will

I am what I am
Not because I am,
But because God made me
What I am.
I will be what I will be
Because God wills me to be,
And because His will be done.

God made me
To know Him
To love Him
And to serve Him
In this world
And the next.

Spring Of Love

Warm and bright
This supernatural light
The spirit of God
Brings the message of eternal life
With its warmth
Radiating beauty everywhere
And calling the chosen
To follow Him in a time
Of awakening growth
Nourishing the good seed
To thrive in the good soil
And giving us victory through
Our lord Jesus Christ.

NY State Fair

By any measure, it was a pleasure

A potpourri of people
Passed my way at the Fair.
They came in all shapes and sizes,
In all different colors and hues.
Some even read today's news.
They laughed and talked,
They ran and walked.
Some stopped to look or eat.
Some came to meet.
Others worked.
While still others sang.
Some marched when bells rang.
I was told
Many things were sold.
So much fun
In rain or sun.
But the best sight by a mile
Was to see so many people smile!

People Watching

I saw a lady at the Fair.
She didn't have any hair.
She had tattoos and earrings everywhere.
Thankfully people watching
Is still free at the Fair.

The Fair Way

We came to see
What's new this year
At the New York State Fair
And we did hear
The sounds of people
Far and near.
We also saw so many sights
Morning, noon
And even at night
Not just the shows that cost
But some free shows that
Last and last
Not just music we liked to hear
But friendly people from far and near
Who showed their arts and crafts
And their animals too.
We saw rabbits, cows and pigs it's true
And horses, birds and sheep.
Some were standing some were asleep.
Other people showed all kinds of plants:
Flowers, shrubs and trees
As well as all kinds of produce that please.
There is no doubt that what's new at the Fair
This year is what's often been there:
It's all the people who really care.

Syracuse University

College Food Service Worker

Running, Stopping
Almost Hopping
Telling, Walking
Sometimes Mopping
Bending, pushing
Taking, Making
Rushing, Brushing
Almost Breaking
Wiping, Cleaning
Looking, Finding
Cooking, Every day.
Sweeping, Washing
Laughing, Crying
Blinking, Thinking.
Very Human Beings.

Dining Hall People

People alive, laughing
Talking, walking
Waiting in line for food.
Thinking, dreaming, loving
Existing, waiting in line
To err but not to always forgive
People wishing at times
To be more than just people.

Last Year's Dream Team

The Final Four
And then more
So much skill
But more than will
The driving force
Behind this team
Was not just one super star:
Wallace
Not just one great coach:
Boeheim,
But it was a brotherhood of players and staff
Caring people united in one cause.
It was a dream team.
Could Syracuse ask for more?

Newhouse Communications Center

Pensive room awaits omnipotent sage.
Sophocles enters and is recognized.
Silence moves with him.
Words exchanged, some in heated debate
Philosophy vs Philosophy
Man-women-sage
Media the message?
Walls set the scene.
Step upon step at NCC A22
Above our world is another and then the daylight.
Is this tomorrow?

Only Ten

Where are they now
The fans that said,
"The football season is over -
The team is dead".
After two games were lost
What did they do?
Yell," Fire the coach"
And boo and boo.
Well the season is over
And real fans had fun
Because the football orange
Have won and won.
(except for Miami)
Let's hope next year
They do as well again.
For with three losses
And a bowl game win
They "only" won ten
So let's hear it for the team
That gave Syracuse good reason
To be proud of the orange
For another football season.

They Gave Their Best

The expectations were low.
How far could they go?
Starters were gone.
Second string to go on. No Top 25.

A time to revive.
Then they started to win.
Again and again they put the ball in.
Allen and Damone
Billy and Deshaun.
And in a great game a blizzard
Of Preston's 3's
That went on and on.

Now the season is over
The ball games are done.
But the Orange finished
With 25 games won.

So let's be thankful
For their hard work and success
And for all the ways
They gave us their best.

S.U.'s Fair Weather Fans

They complain when opponents are too lowly,
And complain when others are too tough.
They complain when starters stay in,
Or when the bench plays it rough.
They complain when Hill fouls out
Or if he doesn't score enough.
They complain if Hart plays injured,
And doesn't have a record game.
They complain if Burgan plays,

Or if on the bench he stays.
They complain if Cipolla can't make every three,
Or if Janulis doesn't do the same.
They complain if the team doesn't make it to the final four
They complain if the team does that and more.
They complain if Coach Boeheim and his staff only win
500 games.
These fair-weather fans will always be the same.
But thankful I am on most every day
For this team and its coaches and for the way
They gave their all and did their part
And for this year,
The year they played with real heart.

One Game Away

SU coach Babers says,
"He wants to be fair."
So many sons
So many players out there.
So many promising youngsters
To help us win:
From a gifted playmaker
To a talented pocket passer to put in
Two skilled but imperfect quarterbacks
With team injuries to overcome.
For now five games have been won
And many fans have been having lots of fun
Because the team is one game away
From a bowl game this year
Whether Dungey or DeVito play more
And we get to cheer
With more wins and a bowl
Why not be fair?

Memories

Another Place

Sleepy
Creepy
I can't keep
My eyes open.
The sandman
Keeps throwing sand
And my hand can't stop
This euphoria of dream-filled
Restfulness
From overwhelming me
And taking m to
Another place.

Lake Thoughts

Silver reflections of a harvest moon
Danced on the waves tonight
And sparkled brightly
As a chilly September wind whistled
Past the lake shore.
Ghost-like clouds passed the silvery moon
Like sailing ships, one at a time
As the sound of wind whipped trees
Echoed across the land.
Nights like this aren't good for swimming
But they are good for sleeping.
Thank God for the beauty of this moment.

Glimpse of the Past

Today my family and I traveled,
For a while, back in time
Along a way built more than a century ago
To a different world, past places other folks
Had not seen in decades.

There were wooded hillsides decked
Out in new spring greenery
And meadow marshlands full of wildlife.
We spotted a beaver hut along with
The many pointed tree stumps they left behind.

We traveled slowly at first so we could
Safely pass crossings.
The loud train whistle let people along the way
Know we were coming. Some bystanders
Waved as we passed and we waved back.

Later we moved faster and the ground by the tracks
Went by in a green blur.
Then we saw a farm or two
And a horse looked up as if to greet us.

Once an abandoned house appeared out of nowhere
And it had trees growing out through a window
But it still showed some of its original well-built beauty
And it made you wonder about the people who had once
lived there.

We stopped at a station called Martisco
And we saw many railroad things that were used long ago.
At a crossroads called Skaneateles Junction.
We paused at another station before our return.

As our train pulled into the Village of Solvay
We thanked our crew
For giving us a glimpse of the past
Even as we traveled along our way to the future.

Saved

Like a surreal forest
In a wasteland
They stand-
An army of tall
Yet broken oak trees

Located in the northwest
Corner of Burnet Park
Along Avery Ave.
With a large X marked
On every other tree.
Can't some be saved?

Like the trees from a world war
With many branches shattered and broken,
Many trunks marred or twisted
Can't some be saved?

Even now some park trees look
Better than street trees
That had their tops cut off
To protect utility wires.
Can't some be saved?

Must we clear cut our natural history
And leave only a memory
Of shade and color, birds and beauty?
Can't some be saved?

I really hope so...

Heavenly View

From high on top of a hill called Myrtle
On a cool fog-filled night
When stars were hidden behind misty clouds
 I could still see many Syracuse sights:
From a dark lakeshore to a valley filled with lights.
There was the mall and the stadium
And over there was downtown and the Dome
And there was the far west side Syracuse neighborhood
So many rows of street lights and homes
So many leafless trees as well as short and tall buildings
Such a misty yet heavenly view
Shared by all the folks from a street
That has homes in Solvay on one side of the street
And homes in Syracuse on the other.

But just at the edge of the blackened wooded hill
A dark furry creature hurries along
Oblivious to people, lights, fog or city noises
As he looks under leaves for a meal confident and strong
Ready to protect himself with a skunk smell
That he usually doesn't have to use.
So I wisely left him alone to go his way
And made a promise to myself
To come back to this spot another day.

Awed

I am awed
By the sacrifices
Of so many everyday people
Who on that day - 9/11/01
And the days that followed
Became real heroes.
So many firefighters, police officers
So many rescue workers and volunteers
Who risked or gave their lives for others.
They were among the first casualties
In this new millennium war against terrorism
Which continues with other victims today.
God, please bless those real American heroes
And their families in the days and years ahead
And help us never to forget their great sacrifices
Even as we say, "God bless America."

Things From the Past

A New Hampshire covered bridge
I walked through a while ago
Made me think back to a time in the past
When horses pulled wagons or sleighs
In sun, rain or snow
As they carried their loads
And transported folks
Along dirt country roads.

Each covered bridge
Has a story to be told
No matter how new
No matter how old
Of people and places
Of times long past
They are reminders
Of things that just last.

One day years and years from now
Strangers will stop
And visit this sight
Of an old covered bridge
In morning or night
As they visit this place from the past
A reminder of things that last and last.

Vermont Covered Bridge

A Vermont covered bridge
I drove through a short time ago
Filled my mind with memories
Of green mountains covered with endless forests
And of valleys filled with multi-colored farmland,
Of clean lakes surrounded by majestic mountains
And of quiet rural roads where friendly people
Can still be found in country stores,
Of busy villages where a church steeple
Is even now the tallest building in town
And of quality hand made products and crafts,
Of a ferry boat ride across a lake called Champlain
But most of all of the special people
Who still call Vermont home.

Still For Sale

They want to close it now
They say it's out of date.
No need for any place
This big or even really this great.

Who wants to live in a place
With a gym, weight room or pool
With an air-conditioned restaurant
And candy store so cool?

Who wants elevators, a theater, a ball field and more?
Who wants a day care, repair garage, apartments galore,
Greenhouse, playgrounds, free parking too?
Commercial kitchens, doctors and nurses for you,
A dentist and police who have rank
Why, it even has a bank.

So if you want a condo with a really nice Syracuse view
Come up to this place and enjoy the good life too.
It's not too late
Because my friend, It once was called S.D.C.
And the landlord was New York State.

Daydreamer

Wandering, wandering what are we to do?
Run away, run away all to start anew
Leaving our troubles behind;
By running away to a new kind
Of life, or only a dream to die;
And shrivel up into nothingness.

Beyond the Moon

A large bright moon that hung by the horizon
In a clear blue winter sky on a recent very cold morning
Was so bright that I could see many of its craters.
It reminded me of an American explorer named Armstrong
Who when he walked on that same moon 47 years ago
Said that he was taking,
"One small step for man one giant leap for mankind".
Perhaps soon Americans will again be inspired
With a renewed vision to return to that heavenly body
And not only walk on the surface but build and explore
In this new world and to even travel beyond…

Election Day

Election day
Tuesday.
We can choose
Or lose.
We can complain
Or act on pain.
We can ignore
Or do more.
We can postpone
And moan.
Or we can rejoice
And make a choice.
Let's vote.

Green Beer

Each spring some people celebrate
Saint Patrick's Day with cheer.
They recall this Christian missionary
Not with prayers but with green beer.
St. Patrick risked his life so others
Could learn about God's word.
He taught Ireland's people
To live and to serve the Lord.
The people built communities with
Christian fellowship and cheer
With many prayers, but not with green beer.
So, when St. Patrick's Day comes again
And you want to be full of good cheer
Ask the Lord to fill you
And pass by the green beer.

© Robert Oberst

Grandpa's Old Red Pump

Grandpa's pump stands proud yet small
Up in the Pompey hills
It doesn't need to be tall.
Sometimes its seals dry out
And they need to be primed, that's all.
Soon cold water comes up from below
So cold it reminds you of last year's snow.
The robins like to stop for a drink
From the tired old pail
And soon Grandpa will go out to the road
And check for the mail.
The corn looks like it's ready to go
Too bad its cow corn, you know.
Fire wood is stacked
And dried by the barn
So it's time to go now
I'm not telling a yarn.

Hunger

Hunger is a physical state,
Not something that can be easily suppressed
Or imagined by the mind.
Hunger is not defined as 24 hours without food.
It is a weak feeling all over your body.
It nibbles at the sides of your stomach.
It wakes you up in the morning
And it says," Good night" when you go to sleep.
It saps your energy and ambition. It slows you down.
It makes you want to sleep endlessly.
But hunger is not always destructive.
It makes you appreciate what you have to eat.
It makes you thankful for a potato or a glass of water.
It makes you realize that poverty is not just a word.
It helps you put some things in perspective
But although you are reminded that
Many of the world's people live and die hungry every day
Your pain continues.
You are thankful to be alive and you are hungry.

Liberate

To free or make free
To conquer in the name of freedom
To replace one form of despotism for another
To free ourselves at the cost of another person's freedom
To reconquer
To "rip off" or steal "justly"
To rape, rob or kill
To destroy in order to "save".
Isn't it time to liberate ourselves from rhetoric?

Just Pass Us By

We don't live near the ocean
We don't live by the sea
But every time it snows
Salt spray washes over me.
Salt hits our house and driveway
It kills our plants and trees
It turns cement to dust
And it washes over everything
As it turns our car to rust.
We wouldn't mind if a salt truck
Came by just when there was ice
But it comes even when there's no snow
And sometimes it comes twice.
So if you drive a salt truck
With salt piled so high,
Please do us a favor
The next time snow
Lightly dusts our street
Save your salt and the public's money
And please just pass us by.

Listen

My head feels like a pressure cooker
With ears plugged, eyes watery
And nose running. My neck and back ache
Just at the edge of a headache my mind
Wonders to God's purpose for me this day.
What is the reason for my suffering?
Time alone with Him?
Time to study what He wants?
Time to read about man, wife and God?
Time to write His words and talk His talk?
But most of all time to listen to Him?

Norwegian Wood

A flute sends notes and feelings
Floating all around my room
Followed by trumpets
And all sorts of other things.
Wood is warm and alive
Even though it was cut long ago.
It comes in browns and reds
Blacks and blonds.
It comes in soft and hard.
In some ways
God made it like people.

Oceans of Love

Oceans of love
Wash over me
Sent from God.
Kind and patient and unfailing
Is this love.
It fills my being
And when I let it flow
It spills over to others -
Here's an ocean for you, Janet.

One of the Greatest

Born in a log cabin February 12, 1809.
Meager schooling, mostly self-taught.
Student of the Bible; man of faith.
Woodsman, blacksmith and fence splitter.
Served in the Army as a volunteer.
Studied the law on his own;
Became one of the best lawyers.
Rugged honesty at the expense of success.
Paramount object: "Save the Union".
Source of moral authority;
People instinctively trusted him.
He said," I want in all cases to do right".
Abraham Lincoln was not only a great
American statesman, but he saved his country
And helped abolish slavery.
He died while in service to his country,
And he should always be remembered
As one of the greatest American heroes.

© Robert Oberst

Remember

Who can remember
Who can recall
The day in November
We scaled the last wall?
The day the war ended
The fighting suspended
Some 100 years ago?
Who can remember
The 11th hour
Of the 11th day
Of the 11th month
When the armistice was signed
And the "war to end all wars"
Came to an end?
So while many soldiers
Still lie in Flanders fields
Few folks remember
Why or when.
It's time once more
To teach our children
That our freedom
Came with a cost
And if we don't remember
It could one day
All be lost.

Smile

A smile that crossed your parted lips
Moved across the room
And surrounded me with joy.
Without warning, it entered my heart
And appeared on my lips.
Later, as I walked down the street,
I saw it pass to another person.
When I see it again
I'll return it to you.

Then

Just as the light was ebbing
A strong breeze lifted willing
Tree branches skyward.
Darkening clouds were
Punctuated by electric flashes,
And wet drops filtered down
Through a jungle of trees. As
Thunder shook the ground
Maple leaves flew across the space
Between here and there,
And then the rains came.

Thanks to the Editor

You didn't hire me
And we don't often agree.
Yet you read my thoughts
On most any day.

You know my imperfections
Such as words I can't spell.
You know when my grammar
Is not quite up to par
Or at least I hope you can tell.

You sometimes print my views
About sunshine or about rain
You even let me criticize you
And at times complain.

So let me pause a minute
To give you year-end thanks
For having room in your paper
For the words of your readers
Even some you think are cranks.

Out of Date

Poetry is out of date
It has no use today.
People rush and people run
And people on their way
Have no use for poetry
Have no time it seems.
Have no use for poetry
Have no time for dreams.
Still I stop to ponder
To think about the world and
To take the time to make a rhyme
And think about even a single pearl.

Year Round Spring Cleaning

Every day
By the side of the road
Some people dump load after load
Of cans and bottles and so much more
Of their unwanted things as they return from the store.
It makes you wonder why they think it's right
To dump their waste on any street, morning noon and night.
Do they toss their cigarette packs everywhere
Or just the spaces where no one seems to care?
Is their car also full of so much trash?
Don't they know deposit cans are worth some cash?
Is the place where they live also full of litter?
And are they really so bitter
About not having a better place to call home
So they drive or walk around tossing trash as they roam?
Why wouldn't they like a road that was clean
Free of fast food wrappers with neighbors not mean?
If you want to live on a more beautiful and clean street
Don't wait for another Earth Day to make it neat.
Ignore those people who don't really care
And do your best with your neighbors to pick up there
As you carry out the true meaning
Of a real neighborhood year round spring cleaning.

Stories

Berliner Mauer

For the last 27 years I have had a three centimeter square block of clear plastic containing a small piece of the "Berliner Mauer" (Berlin Wall).

The wall was first constructed in 1961 by the German Democratic Republic (East Germany). This government which was not democratic nor was it a republic but rather it was a totalitarian communist dictatorship. The wall was built to keep the people of East Germany imprisoned. On June 26, 1963 President John F. Kennedy came to Berlin and said, "All free men are citizens of free Berlin." He also defended freedom for the people of the city by saying, "Ich bin ein Berliner."

On June 12, 1987 president Ronald Reagan came to Berlin and said, "If you seek peace, Mr. Gorbachev, tear down this wall."

On November 9,1989 restrictions on the free movement of the people of East Berlin were lifted and it was the beginning of the end of the cold war as well as the beginning of the reunification of a free and democratic Germany.

The Berlin wall and even a small piece of it is a reminder of the importance of freedom and its cost to people willing to support real democracy in a real republic.

I want to take a moment to recall your life and to thank you for being my father. It was decades ago, just before World War II, that you fell in love with Mom and you gave up your independent life to be committed in marriage to her. You gave yourself to your family and to your country in spite of hardships, years of separation and life-threatening military service in the Pacific.

After the war, you worked what seemed like endless hours to support our growing family. Many nights you only had a few hours' sleep. Your determined efforts made our lives better and the love you shared with Mom and your five children made our lives special. You weren't a perfect dad and we weren't perfect children, yet when you and I had disagreements I was always confident of your love. Thanks for that love even when I hurt or disappointed you.

Over the years you gave your children many gifts. You supplied our material needs first when times were hard (when six of us lived in a three-room third-floor Bronx apartment) and to make things better, you worked three jobs first with the N.Y. National Guard, then with the New York Telephone Company and you also did television repair. Your efforts made it possible for us to move into our own suburban home. You and Mom worked, sacrificed and saved to give all your children a chance to better ourselves and even go to college.

You taught us all to work hard for a goal - whether it is a family, job or even a hobby. You guided my interests in such things as gardening, Model "A" Fords, history, photography and community service. But the best gift you gave your children was the continuing love you had for Mom in good times and bad.

It's been over twenty years since you went on to meet your maker but the memory of your life is still strong in the hearts of your family. Thanks, Dad.

When I look back to the Christmases of my childhood, certain memories fill my mind. I remember, as a twelve year old, going with my dad late on Christmas Eve to a New York City railroad yard to get our family's Christmas tree right off a freight car to get the lowest price.

We decorated our tree just like my German grandparents decorated their tree. We made strips of colored paper into ring chains and paper lanterns. We threaded popcorn into long chains.

We cut out pictures from old Christmas cards and hung them on the tree. And we put metal tinsel all over the branches. At the top of the tree there was a large white star. We even had a few handmade wooden ornaments from "the old country" along with some child-made decorations we created ourselves.

Then there were the lights. They were large and if one light in the chain burned out, all the lights went out. Some of the lights almost looked like real candles. The tree took up a lot of space in our small, three-room Bronx apartment, but the four of us children didn't mind at all because it was Christmas.

At school and at church we were reminded of the connection between Christmas and the giving of gifts to others.

The manger placed under the tree had no Christ Child until Christmas morning so we recalled why we celebrated the day.

I don't know how my parents did it with our limited family income, but on Christmas morning there was a pile of gifts under our tree for all of us and once there was even a special train set for me. At church we celebrated the birth of Jesus, our gift from God.

Many Christmases have come and gone since then, but the special memories remain. After the gift of the Christ Child, the best gift we received was the love and self-sacrifice of our parents at Christmas and all through the years in good times and hard times. Although my parents have years ago gone to meet their maker, the gift of their example remains fresh in their children's memories, especially at Christmas.

© Robert Oberst

Labor Day Storm memory: I saw only darkness

At about 1:20 a.m. on Labor Day (9/7/98), I woke up and heard loud thunder and a strange wind sound. I looked out a window and saw only darkness.

All the street lights were out, and the sound of heavy rain on everything filled the darkness. After gathering the family together downstairs we brought out the flashlights and our transistor radio and listened to the news.

It was a storm to remember. After checking out the family I discovered that the 100-year-old maple tree in front of our house was resting on our roof a few inches from our 6-year-old daughter's bedroom window. The family was safe, the house was dry, but the roof was damaged.

When the wind and rain ended, I set out like a good Neighborhood Watch member on foot with my flashlight and my cellphone. A neighbor and I cleared some large tree branches from our dark street, but we stayed clear of the downed wires at the end of the block. A few individuals insisted on driving their cars back and forth on a few clear streets but they gave up when they saw that they couldn't go anywhere.

Several streets even had electricity for an hour or so, and some people came out to clear paths and assess damage. It was hard to get 911, but one neighbor got through to NiMo to ask them to fix a gas leak caused by two fallen trees near a broken utility pole and a car turned on its side.

Neighbors on darkened streets checked to see who needed help, who needed to make calls because of no phone service, who needed flashlights, etc. Soon all the lights went out on the last few neighborhood streets and everyone went back inside. The radio announcers gave us information on what was happening all over Central New York.

For the next seven days, although we did have land-line telephone service, our house was lit at night by the glow of several old gas lamps and we cooked our meals on our backyard grill. We knew that we had many things to be thankful for, yet our neighborhood was forever changed.

Many of our oldest, most beautiful trees were gone or soon to be cut down. It was many months before most neighborhood roofs were repaired, and some buildings were demolished. But some neighbors were re-acquainted, and relationships were strengthened. The following years new trees were planted along some area streets for the next generation of neighbors to appreciate and to help build a stronger, more attractive community.

In the years following WWII, our family of six lived in a three-room third floor Bronx apartment. We had no garden, but I often spent time watching my grandfather, the building caretaker, cut the hedges around the building. At the age of eleven, my spending money came from my returning two and three cent deposit bottles to grocery stores or "fishing" for lost coins with chewing gum on a stick down sidewalk grates. A few weeks before Mother's Day I knew what I wanted to give my mom. I had saved mostly pennies for her gift.

A few days before Mother's Day I went to a flower store and I asked the clerk how much it cost for a single red rose. He asked me how much money I had. I counted out ninety nine cents and he said, "That's just right".

My mother was delighted with her gift, yet she reminded me that since I was born on her first Mother's Day that I was her most precious Mother's Day gift.

My Pet

I'm sure growing up in America's largest city has always been a challenge. In the "baby boom" years following WWII most of New York City schools were packed with children of many backgrounds and nationalities. In the Bronx parochial school I attended as a twelve year old we had "split sessions" where one nun taught seventy boys in the morning, with the help of a small ruler, and then she taught seventy girls in the afternoons. My week days were filled at home with homework but with four children in our three-room, third floor apartment there were few quiet spots.

For me free time was spent playing in the "woods" (otherwise known as empty lots!) or playing street games such as stickball or even a travel game of ride the subway back and forth. Donald, my best friend, and I spent a lot of free time together. Although he was born in Puerto Rico he spoke little Spanish and he had thick blond hair. We spent many Saturdays exploring areas of our Bronx neighborhood. Once I pulled Donald out of "quicksand" located in some Bronx River swampland and "saved his life" or so he said. One of our best adventures happened on the day we walked many blocks to Pelham Bay Park to look for some fish. Along the shore of Long Island Sound we saw a fisherman pull in an eel. He was upset that the eel was all tangled up in his line. We asked him for the eel so he cut his line and he gave us the snake-like fish. After unwinding the remaining line from around the eel and removing the hook from its mouth we placed it in an old water-filled can. Then we rushed back to my family's apartment. Quickly we filled the bathtub with cold water and put the eel in it. At last I had a pet! My sister, Muffet, on her way to take a bath, discovered my pet and started yelling. My mother immediately gave away my pet to our neighbors in the next apartment. I suspect they ate it for supper. It was a long time before I had another pet.

The times were different. Manlius was a small town then. There were many farms at the outskirts of the village. The Manlius Theater was so small there were only four seats on each side of the aisle. Edwards Falls was a special spot for a long walk in the woods. Lipe's Dairy had the best ice cream for miles and Suburban Park was a great place to go for a cool roller coaster ride on a hot summer day.

© Robert Oberst

Just outside the village stood the beautifully landscaped campus of The Manlius School. The school was called St. John's Academy until the 1920's when the name was changed to The Manlius School. As a military academy for approximately 300 boys from grades 7-12 the school had extensive grounds and athletic fields, a large chapel-auditorium, an academic building, an infirmary, a dining hall, barber shop and even a snack bar called the Phoenix Tavern. The school prepared boys for college and/or military careers. Academic classes, sports activities, and military training were important parts of the school program. As a college prep military school the campus was run like a military post. Most high school students lived at school in one of three dormitories with their "companies". There was "A", "B", "C", and "HQ". Various military uniforms were worn at all times. There were uniforms for class, for rain or snow, for work or sports and for "dress" occasions. Military haircuts were standard. All students and teachers had military rank. Academic classes covered many college prep subjects from Latin or German to Algebra or speed reading in addition to PT (Physical Training) as well as M.S.T. (Military Science and Tactics). There was a demerit system used to help control student behavior. Repeated incidents of any student caught smoking in a school building resulted in their expulsion. I only attended The Manlius School for one year, 1958-1959 (my junior year.) Due to my father's job transfers, my family moved several times while I was in high school so I attended three very different schools over my four years of high school. While this experience had many disadvantages, it gave me some unique insights on comparing schools and pinpointing the role that The Manlius School played in my life. I'm sure every Manlius cadet who marched past Comstock Hall has unique memories of his student days and so I cannot speak for them but rather I can only recall, with strong yet imperfect memories what those days meant to me.

My first days as a new Manlius student were a lot like joining the Army: haircuts, uniforms, no civilian clothes, rules and more rules, no social life and plenty of marching drills. Veteran students knew the rules and had some kind of rank. I was a "private" and everyone with "rank" was above me. I was assigned to "B" company. I soon learned the "B" Company marching songs, played on the "B" Company intramural sports teams and was proud to be part of "B" Company.

Once classes started, our weekdays fell into a regular routine. Up and dressed at dawn, we stood in formation with our company outside for reveille. Then we returned to our rooms to make our beds, etc. When we returned to our formation the entire student body watched the flag go up the pole and then we marched to the mess hall for breakfast. We sat with fellow members of our company with the highest ranking cadet at the head of each table. Each private had to take turns being bus boy for the day which meant he waited on two tables. Meal time was not always serious. One morning we marched into the mess hall to find a teacher's compact car in the middle of the dining area with our dining table all around it. Then there was the day when the head of our table was dishing out spaghetti and he found a dead mouse in it so our table fasted for that meal.

Our classes were small and demanding. Our tests were always harder than Regents exams. One very strong memory of my first day of school was English 11 class. The classroom was full of students. The highest ranking cadet called the class to attention when our teacher, Captain Marsh, came into the room. Captain Marsh said, "At ease." Then he said, "Before this academic year is over, half of you will fail this class." Some students laughed but by the end of the year we saw that he was correct. Most of my classes were not as intense but a good deal of learning went on in them. I especially enjoyed Mr. Bisgrove's speed reading class. It has served me well since that time. After classes were over for the day, we had many activities such as intramural sports, clubs and various tasks. I really enjoyed rifle club, planting trees in the forestry club with Mr. Shaw and helping a friend in the school greenhouse. We could entertain guests on weekends and enjoy free time at the Phoenix Tavern. There were social events and dances but these were expensive. Across the road from our campus was an amusement park called Suburban Park. One day a year our whole school was invited to go to the Park exclusively. The rest of the Park was off limits. I enjoyed walks up to Lipe's Dairy for an ice cream as often as I was permitted to go.

Classes in Military Science and Tactics were an important part of our education at The Manlius School. More than book learning we had to learn to disassemble an M-1 rifle and then reassemble it in the dark. We had many field exercises such as the day our squad advanced in two groups across a smoke filled football field to an "enemy" target. We had M-1s with blanks and the "enemy" had a machine gun with blanks. Not a game - we were graded on our battle.

Many of our Saturdays were spent marching: marching to meals, marching to church, marching to improve our marching or marching so that "B" Co. could be the "Honor" Company in the year end competition. Other Saturdays were spent in white glove inspections of our rooms, our uniform and our M-1's. We spent plenty of time spit polishing our boots and shoes so they looked like glass and making the blankets on our beds so tight a quarter would bounce on them.

At the end of some very long days there was lights out time but I still had school work to do so I used to study under my blanket with a flashlight.

It was with great pride, at the end of my year at Manlius, that our entire school in our best 'A' uniforms marched behind our color guard and our own HQ band in the May 1959 Syracuse Memorial Day parade.

Looking back, my year at The Manlius School helped me to build self-confidence and showed me the value of academic as well as physical hard work. High academic demands pushed me even past some failures to work at greater intensity. Physical training where all students were mandated to participate in intramural teams and military training also built my confidence and physical abilities. My year at Manlius gave me a better understanding of my father and his years of military service. It also gave me some of the tools I greatly needed to graduate from college and complete my military service. I can even credit Manlius for my appreciation for marching bands, neatness and Central N.Y.

© Robert Oberst

Blizzard Power of Love

What's a mere blizzard against the power of love and a faithful Volkswagen?

It was Jan. 28 1977. I was looking forward to a weekend visit with my girlfriend, Janet, at D'Youville College in Buffalo. The trip from my Syracuse apartment usually took about three hours on the N.Y. State Thruway. I left work an hour early, at 2 pm. A local radio announcer said that a snowstorm with high winds was moving across the state from the west and the Thruway was closed between Buffalo and Syracuse. My 1965 Volkswagen ("Betsy Bug") had new tires, and it liked to go in the snow. It wasn't snowing in Syracuse. So I filled the car with gas and drove west on Route 5 to Auburn. A few miles farther, now on Route 20, I encountered a white-out, my first real taste of the storm. Blowing snow made it hard to see more than a few feet in front of the car. Traffic slowed down to a crawl. My wind-shield wipers couldn't keep up with the heavy snow so I pulled over to the side of the road to clean off my windshield. A little further down the road, I saw the three cars that had been following me before I pulled over. They had bumped into one another due to the poor visibility. The air was so cold that the snow came down in beads and bounced off my windshield without my wipers on. The wind grew in intensity, and the snow started to form drifts. Although the wind chill was below zero, I had some heat in my car and the road was passable, so I continued west at a steady speed. After about an hour I came to an intersection on Route 20 that had a three-foot snow drift in it. I knew that I couldn't get through it, so I parked my car with the engine running in a space between two parked tractor trailers whose drivers were waiting for a plow to come. As I sat in my VW, I wondered how long I would have enough gas to keep my car warm. I also wondered if it had been such a good idea to pick this weekend to go to Buffalo.

After what seemed like a long wait, I finally said a prayer, asking God to help me. Within a short time, a pickup truck with a short plow blade and a car passed by me and I quickly pulled out to follow them. We went together on through the snow for many miles. I later found out that this enterprising pickup truck driver was on his way to plow out Buffalo streets and there were about 30 cars behind my "little bug" in our convoy. As it grew dark, I thought that the pickup would plow me through to Buffalo in a short time. But we started up a small hill and the snow was too deep to plow uphill, so the truck driver lifted his blade. The car behind him got stuck. I couldn't pass him so our little "convoy" was forced to stop.

Within about a half an hour a large volunteer fire department van from a place called Attica came to pick up the stranded drivers and took us to a local firehouse. At the firehouse I heard from some of the other drivers that my VW had been a kind of flagship for our "convoy" these drivers had told one another to "follow the bug". I called Janet in Buffalo to let her know that I was safe and then I slept on an army cot in the fire hall. Early the next morning, the snow had let up and the roads were passible. The pickup driver had spent the night at the fire hall and I followed him the short distance on

Route 20 to Buffalo. I was amazed at what I saw. City streets were clogged with snow drifts and with disabled cars on both sides of the street. After I arrived at D'Youville at about noon that Saturday, I heard on the radio that all non-emergency traffic had had been ordered off Buffalo streets by 3 p.m. so the streets could be plowed. It was reported that the college would be closed all week so Janet and two of her friends packed their clothes and we drove back to Syracuse with no problem.

For many people that weekend will always be remembered as the Blizzard of '77, but for me it will be the special weekend when it took 22 hours to get to Buffalo in my VW bug to visit the very special person who would later become my wife. To those who would ask me if I would do that trip again and whether I would risk myself again to see the woman I still love, my answer is, "yes, I would". I might go with a bit more preparation and a bit more experience, but I would go. Was I at least a little foolhardy to try such a trip? Yes. But my experience, over 40 years ago, taught me how really dependent I was not on luck but on the grace of God to get me through difficult circumstances. I also reaffirmed my belief in the power of even a simple prayer.

About the Author

Robert L. Oberst was born in The Bronx, New York in 1942. He lived with his family of six in a modest three room third floor apartment. His father, Lee Oberst, worked many jobs to support his growing family from the New York State National guard, the New York Telephone Company and a job fixing radios and televisions. He also attended college night school. His mother Alice Oberst worked very hard caring for her four children (later to be five). She passed her love of reading to her children.

In order for his father to advance in his telephone company job the Oberst family had to move a number of times. In 1954 they moved to Westchester County and in 1957 they moved to Oneida County. By 1959 they returned to Westchester. Robert attended three very different high schools over those years: Edgemont High School, Whitesboro High School and The Manlius (Military) School. After graduation from Edgemont, Oberst attended New England College in New Hampshire and he graduated with a BA in History in 1964. He then joined the U.S. Army where after extensive training he served as a Special Agent in Army Intelligence.

In 1969 Oberst attended graduate school at Syracuse University and he did volunteer work at a number of city elementary schools. For the next thirty-five years starting in 1970's Oberst worked in the special education field at the Syracuse Developmental Center and various community locations.

Over the 40 years Bob Oberst lived in Syracuse with his remarkable wife and his wonderful family, he has participated in many family friendly activities and volunteered for many area functions. In 1985 Bob joined Neighborhood Watch Groups of Syracuse. In 1989 he helped to organize the Far West Tipp Neighborhood Association and Watch Group. This group is still active on the far west side neighborhood. Bob also serves on the city-wide Neighborhood Watch Group board.

© Robert Oberst

He joined the Men's (now Men's and Women's) Garden Club of Syracuse in 1987 and served on its board for a number of years. He still volunteers on the "Zoo Crew" doing gardening work once a week at the Burnet Park Zoo. Bob is also a member of the Solvay Neighborhood Watch Group.

He has been a member and facilitator of the west side TNT (Tomorrow's Neighborhoods Today) for a number of years. He served as a tree steward wherever curb side trees needed work.

Bob has done a variety of garden projects in a number of Syracuse neighborhood locations from Syracuse Developmental Center, to Lewis Park, to Saint Patrick's School, to the CMA Church and to Faldo Park.

He is also a member of the Tipperary Hill Association and he participates in many of their activities. He worked with the members of the West End Little League and a number of other people in the neighborhood to clean up and restore Lewis Park and to acquire N.Y. State grants to rebuild its concession building as well as planting many trees and potted flowers along area streets. Over the years Bob and his family participated in many neighborhood sports and volunteer school activities.

CPSIA information can be obtained
at www.ICGtesting.com
Printed in the USA
BVHW050441250322
632222BV00002B/5